BAT PENDER

The BEST SUSPENDER in the world that you can make yourself!

By Ron Battiston

Your first reaction and that would be very understandable, is "What the hell is a Bat Pender?" I actually invented something that works a lot better than a standard set of suspenders which millions of people have been using for hundreds of years to help them prevent their pants from falling down. Nobody wants their pants to fall down because that tends to show body parts we normally keep private. I have decided to share my invention because I know that it will help lots of people and because I think that the BAT PENDER works a lot better than a pair of suspenders for a lot less money! In fact you can make them yourself in about 15 minutes for usually under $10.

This booklet is about an inexpensive yet very effective alternative to a standard set of suspenders. I invented the BAT PENDER in 2018 probably by accident. Remember, the main purpose of a set of suspenders is to keep your pants from falling down. That could be embarrassing. You may fill your pockets up with your wallet and change and your car and house keys and other stuff and guess what happens. Your pants start to fall down even if you are wearing a belt. This applies to both men and women. So what you do is grab the top of your pants and pull them back up. Surely there is a better way and trust me I discovered it!

My invention was much to my surprise. You don't need to purchase them from China you can make them yourself while having fun doing it and while spending much less than on a standard set of suspenders. It took me about 15 minutes to make mine and I am not a professional with a needle and thread.

In my youth I was lucky enough to attend and even graduate from one of Canada's best Universities. I wasn't rich and had to work at full time jobs at the same time! One of the many ideas that I learned at University was that you can "think outside the box" and when you do that you sometimes discover something that was not present inside the box! And most of the time people just think you are crazy! Maybe I am.

Standard suspenders are definitely "inside the box" and people have been using them for hundreds of years. Their design has not changed much. In manufacturing when folks discover a good design they keep on building it. But then somebody comes up with an even better idea. As strange as it sounds this is what is happening here.

So what I am doing here is explaining in detail how you can make this invention for your own use at a very low cost that you will find very useful. I think that you will also enjoy making it! We spend way too much time watching TV, playing on the computer and using our cell phones these days. When you make something you usually have a lot of fun, you are proud of what you have completed and you have something that will last for years and not only that you save a lot of money that would otherwise go to big companies and into taxes for governments.

In fact, this device is so useful that you may even make them for your family members and friends as really cool gifts and you could even make them as a hobby and make a few dollars selling them on Kijiji, eBay and swap shops! There is real potential here!

The actual instructions take only a few pages and so I have included some additional information that I hope that you will find interesting and entertaining too!

I hope that you enjoy this booklet.

Cheers!

Ron Battiston

This is a picture of the **BAT PENDER** *which is so small that you can place it inside the strap of a watch. And it works better than a standard suspender works! And it is easy to make if you follow our directions!*

Let me start by saying that this booklet is all about how to make what I am calling the "BAT PENDER" which I invented and which works much better than a standard suspender. You might ask why did I call it a "BAT PENDER"? Good question!

I had to call it something! I couldn't call it a "suspender" because it didn't look or act like a suspender. My first name is Ron so I couldn't call it "Ron's Suspender" I thought of several names like Magic Pender, Single Pender, Genius Pender, Best Suspender and Beaver Pender and others came to mind. I decided on BAT PENDER because it sounded sort of neat and the device was pretty neat and it worked very well. And there is another advantage with this name. If somebody sees you wearing this device they will often ask you " What is that?" And all you need to say is "It's a **BAT PENDER** and I made it myself". Trust me- that will result in a very friendly conversation and you will both enjoy it! They will be impressed with you and you can both have fun! It sounds a lot better than saying "It's made in China and I bought it at Walmart."

Not only do I show you in detail how to make your own BAT PENDER there is also a good story here and so what I will do is tell you more about suspenders and how our economy works today then provide you with detailed information on how you can easily make a BAT Pender that will work surprising better than standard suspenders. The basic reason for suspenders is that pants tend to fall down. That could be embarrassing and

annoying. So here we go with
our story.

ALL ABOUT SUSPENDERS

Standard suspenders are available
at several quality levels starting
around $15 USD to just over
$100 USD. Then you add tax and
shipping. But you can build the
BAT PENDER for under $10
USD and it works even better and
lasts a lot longer too!

There are millions of people in
the world that have exactly the
same problem with pants or
shorts. They tend to fall down. So
in an attempt to solve that
problem they use belts and tighten
the belt so that the clothing won't
fall down. But guess what? In

most cases the pants fall down anyway! Let's consider why. Why do your pants fall down? Possibly not all the way but far enough that people behind you can see the top of your bum!

The average person's waist is the narrowest part of their abdomen EXCEPT if they are overweight. And millions of people are overweight. And strangely, depending on the design of the pants, even skinny people have a problem with their pants slipping down. But your belt is normally placed around your waist. Yes there are some exceptions because some people do not wear belts but most people do. Belts vary in price and quality. You can buy a cheap belt made in China for under $10 and it might last you a couple of years. You can also purchase a very expensive belt possibly made in Europe or the USA or Canada for around $100 that will last a life time. Or if you had tons of money you could purchase a very high quality high end belt like the ones that Gucci in Italy make for $500 or even more and they would last a lifetime. But in a way there is one thing that happens no matter how much you pay for your belt. What if you move?

And here is what happens when you move. The belt tends to slide down because the dimension of your body under your gut are often a bit less than where your navel is. So what happens is that when the belt slides down to an area with less diameter the belt is looser and your pants slip down. So there you are walking around in public trying with one hand to keep your pants up! Traditionally there was a solution to this. Suspenders! In Great Britain they call them Braces. They have been around for hundreds of years and you might think that by now the design is so well developed that there are no problems with them. That would be incorrect. Often the damn suspenders don't work that well. Especially the cheap ones made mostly in China.

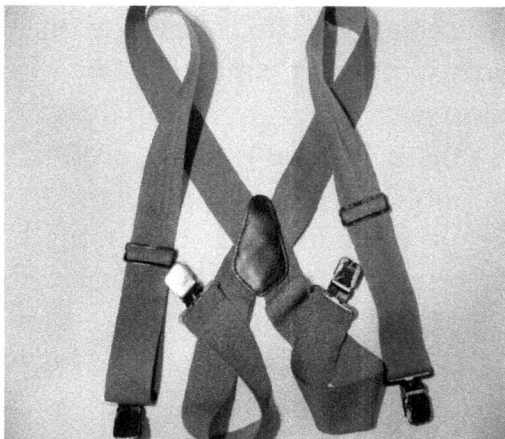

As you can see these traditional suspenders look pretty ugly and what do you suppose happens when you put them on? You look pretty ugly too!

Your suspenders consisted of two belts which were often elastic with metal clamps on each end and crossing at the back. So the the belt on your lower right would travel up over you right shoulder and to down at an angle at the back to the left side your your belt at the back. The other belt would do the same and the two belts would cross at the back and be fastened to each other. At the end of each belt there would be a metal clamp which would fasten onto either your belt or your pants. Sometimes a leather flange with button holes would also be used but then you would need buttons on your pants to attach them. Did they work? Yes and no. It was the No part that got me and I decided to try and fix the problems.

I should tell you a little bit about me first. I am one of three brothers and when we grew up our Mom told us "that there was no such word as can't". So if something didn't work we never gave up. We all graduated from University and all had successful careers. We were lucky but we also worked hard and when somebody said "you can't do that" we did it anyway! At the places I worked I discovered things that nobody else seemed to notice and every place I worked I was promoted. I am not bragging just telling you what happened. And yes I am sure they thought I was a bit nuts too. If they see that I invented the BAT PENDER they will be convinced that I am nuts! I also owned my own businesses and again I was one of those lucky people who seemed able to solve problems. My theory is that I seem to think outside the box a lot. And I understand that often others will think you are a bit nuts when you don't use standard practices (inside the box) to live and enjoy life. And that takes us to suspenders.

I have owned several pairs of suspenders over the years. And the problem was that the clamps would slide off and also the suspender looked so big that they changed the appearance of your clothing. And they weren't that comfortable either. Sometimes when you sat down the metal clamps would rub against your skin. So I decided I would invent a better suspender and that is when something FANTASTIC happened! And I am sharing it with you. I admit that I really wasn't expecting what happened. I even did some research to see if the idea had been invented before and I also did some research about suspenders. Much to my surprise I could not find anyone who had discovered what I did. That seemed so strange given that suspenders have been around for hundreds of years and have been worn by millions of people and yet there is such a simple solution that works much better!

So people have been wearing suspenders for hundreds of years! Why didn't somebody come up with my invention years and years ago? Yes there was some variations in design. Some had metal clips. Some had elastic webbing. Some had nylon webbing. Some were adjustable. Some had leather fasteners where buttons were required on your pants. Some would work with or without belts. Some had only one belt attached to to back of your pants with two belts coming over your shoulders.

The webbing material varied a bit too. Some of it was quite expensive. Over the years at times belts were worn or not worn and pants were loose or tight and rode high or low over or under your waist. Some suspenders were very strong such as the ones used by firefighters or lumberjacks.

The official documented inventor of suspenders was Albert Thurston and he did that just about 200 years ago when pants tended not to have belts and were quite high over the waist region. I am sure that people were wearing them before Albert took his design to the patent office but apparently he was the official suspender inventor. Honestly I don't believe he was because people wore suspenders before Albert was born. The first US Patent for suspenders was obtained by Samuel Clement who was also the Author of Mark Twain. People considered suspenders to be a form of underwear that shouldn't be seen so there was a tendency to switch over to belts. And as I pointed out we have a problem with belts and people with a bit of extra weight because their darn pants still tend to slip down.

As time marched on suspenders were worn by well known individuals like Larry King on TV, by certain musicians and even by certain types of people. Even women wore them to keep their pants and skirts and even their stockings up. At the same time in the upper crust it was considered wrong in some areas to wear both the belt and suspenders at the same time. They had a lot of rules in our upper societies.

Now here is a problem. If you wear suspenders nobody will notice if you place something over them like a shirt or sweater. However you cannot place those items inside your pants because the suspenders are in the way.

Placing a sweater over them is OK. It is much easier to hide a Bat Pender than a suspender!

Traditional suspenders are messy and take a lot of space when you pack.

Now that is your introduction into suspenders from a historical and performance point of view. Millions of people wore suspenders and still do today.

Manufacturers and retail stores made billions of dollars making and selling them. And I think I will add one more thing about that. I have nothing against those who operate a business and I have done that myself over many years. But I do not like the concept of running a business to rip people off. So here goes.

When China started to take over the world's manufacturing market they pulled a dirty trick. And they got away with it. What was it you ask? They made suspenders that could be sold at a significantly cheaper costs than manufacturers in the UK, Europe, the United States and Canada. Why do you suppose they did this and guess what happened?

Those manufacturers went out of business. And guess where most of the suspenders are made today? But that is not all the story. And China does this with almost everything they make. They make the suspenders to look good but not to last long. For example the metal they use for clip holders often bends because it is too thin and often rusts and the clips are cheaply made and often stretch or break. So instead of buying one pair of suspenders for say 15 or more years of use you buy three pairs of suspenders for five or less years of use each. Yes their products are cheaper but they don't last as long and so you need to buy more of them. So your total costs over the years that you use them are actually higher than buying one good quality pair at the start!

It gets even more complicated and I will share that too. Often a company in China will buy a company in North America that is making some product that they wish to compete with. Remember they are not planing for annual production like North American factories they are looking decades ahead. They then close down the factory and move the equipment to China where they produce the same product at a much lower cost because of lower labor and business expenses and then they ship the product back to the stores in North America. And now they have no competition in America because they closed down all the plants competing with them and moved the equipment to China.

It is not just suspenders we are talking about all sorts of consumer products. I noticed this for the first time while I was at University and worked on an afternoon shift at a famous once Canadian tool factory (Beaver Tools) in Guelph Ontario. It had been purchased by an American company (the name changed to Rockwell Beaver) who built excellent quality tools there for decades. Then guess what happened? A Chinese company purchased the American company then closed down the factory and moved all the production tools to China and guess where the tools are made now? Today, decades after I worked at this tool plant I still see "Rockwell Beaver" tools around and when I do I check them out to see if I had made any of the parts. I don't do that when I see equipment made in China. I think it is so important for our labour market to be proud of the tools and machinery and products they make and this is one of the reasons I wrote this booklet. You CAN build products here in North America and be proud of it too. There CAN be good jobs for future generation IF we continue to keep a fair share of production here.

Foreign manufacturers do the same tings with pens and so many other things they make. Let me give you another example of that problem. The UK once made high quality china plates and knives from Shefield they lasted for decades. Then China came along and made much cheaper plates and knives built to a lower quality that still looked good. They put the UK manufacturers out of business and now instead of buying one set of dishes or kitchen knives they will sell you several sets that wear out over you life

The reason that I am telling you all this is that I am going to show you how you can make your own BAT Pender that will avoid this low quality problem that China has been dumping on world markets for decades. And to be very clear I have nothing against China! I love Chinese food and know some great Canadians with Chinese heritage. I think China has done an excellent job making products and taking over world manufacturing. They have been very successful. They have even increased their quality standards usually after they take over a market. But what I am focused on is supporting manufacturing in your home countries. I really think that people in each country should make some of the products they use every day not depend on other countries for everything. So lets move on to how I arrived at this new design.

Out of pure luck I tried a new design for what I thought would be a suspender and it worked perfectly. I discovered that if you built the suspender with just ONE belt and if you designed it correctly it would work even better than a standard suspender with two belts and metal clips. How did I do that? I just thought outside the box and there it was!

Me and the Bat Pender were outside that box and you can be there too with your Bat Pender. You suddenly won't be the same as everyone else and there are some advantages to this.

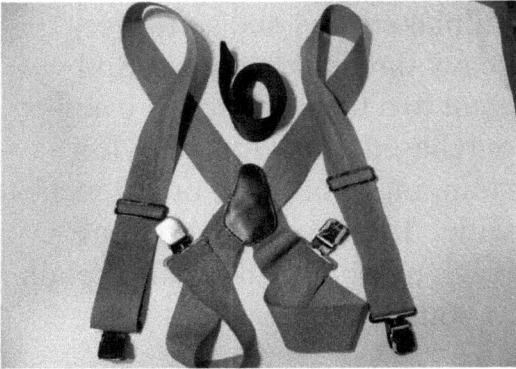

Here is the traditional suspender in red looking terrible and in the middle top in black you will also see a BAT PENDER that works even better! Notice how tiny the BAT PENDER is.

I once lived on a sailboat. It was 56 feet overall and about 40 feet on deck with a ketch rig. One thing that you need to understand on a sailboat is how to repair a tear in a sail. For that you need a sailmakers awl and some very heavy thread. I had that. So I went to a local fabric store and purchased a few feet of nylon strapping about 4cm or 1.5 inches wide. I had some very strong black nylon thread. I will explain to you exactly how to do this.

All you need to do is read the actual directions and follow them to the letter. They are not difficult and trust me you will be surprised and very happy with the results.

DETAILED INSTRUCTIONS ON HOW TO MAKE THE BAT PENDER.

STEP ONE

1.

Get all the material that you need to proceed including:

a. a pair of scissors

b. 5 or 6 feet of nylon 4 cm (1.5") webbing

c. a bic lighter or some matches

d. a strong needle capable of going through the webbing

e. a few feet of very strong black thread

f. a piece of heavy cardboard about 2" to 2 ½ inches wide and about four inches wide

g. a good place to work

h. a measuring tape.

When you are collecting this material make sure that the thread really is heavy duty. Nylon is the best material. As far as the sewing needle goes for some strange reason it is very easy to sew through two layers of nylon belt and so you don't really need a sailmakers awl but of course if you have one you can use that too. In the photo you can see a glass of water and that is just in case you start a small fire with the match as you melt the end of the nylon belt. Just stick it into the glass of water! When that stuff starts to burn it melts and you don't want that on your skin. You would hate me if that happened so there is your warning. There is an advantage to a lighter vs a match because with a match you need to be careful the darn match doesn't burn down to your fingers.

STEP TWO

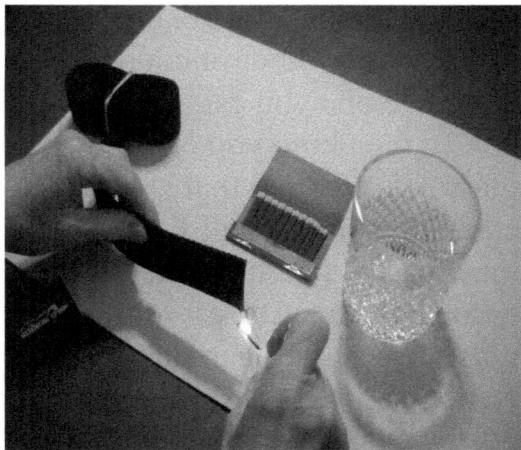

The first thing you need to do is take the end of the webbing and treat it carefully with a lighter or match or even a candle to ensure that the end of the webbing won't fray. What happens here is that the nylon melts slightly so that it does not come apart at the end. You don't want the darn belt to catch on fire and it might be a good idea to have a glass of water handy just in case. And before you melt the edge of the belt be sure that it is cut at a 90 degree angle to the length of the belt not at an angle. This steps should only take you a few seconds. But for pete sakes remember that when you are working with a flame even a small one you need to take care. Have a glass of water handy and work in a safe area.

Safety is an issue here so be careful. Why am I so sensitive to fire? In my Navy days we all trained as firefighters and we understand fires. Trust me. Fires and grow very fast and hurt you very much. That glass of water in the photo is there for that reason. After you have completed the work on the webbing you can add some rum to the water.

STEP THREE

3.

Take that small piece of cardboard and place it at the end of the belt then bend the end of the belt around the cardboard. What you have just done is make a loop approximately 2" wide. Pretty simple eh? This should take you about five seconds.

STEP FOUR

4.

Now you take your needle and place about 3 feet of thread in it and then tie a knot at the end. So you should have about 1.5 feet of two lines of thread with a knot at the end. This might take you a minute but now you are ready to sew! You will find that the needle goes through the webbing very easily. If not you could use a

small set of pliers or even a cork
to push the needle through.

STEP FIVE

5.

Starting on the same side as the
loop meets the belt start to sew
the loop to the belt. Sew about
$1/8^{th}$ of an inch or slightly more
from the edge and gradually sew
across the belt until you have
several thread loops thru the belt
thus holding the belt loop
securely in place. This might take
you about five minutes.

You need to be careful because
you want the thread to go entirely
through each time and you want it
to look neat. Once you have done

that you are half done! Just be sure to do it well. The strong thread that you are using will add strength to the loop with each stitch and you can go across the belt a couple of times to do a good job. And go right to the edge and back. When you have done that try and secure the last stitch with a knot so that it won't come lose. Now remember that step FIVE is important. You do not want these loops to come loose. And if you do a good job sewing them they won't. They could be there forever thanks to you!

STEP SIX

6.

I will call step six a *CRITICAL STEP*. Your objective is to get the length of the BAT PENDER belt correct. So here is how to do it. It may sound silly but it works. Put your pants on and place the completed look on the back of the belt to the right side of your spine. I would say about two inches. You don't want it all the to the right side you want in on your back side.

Now the next step is to take the other end of the belt and lift it over your right shoulder and run it down to your belt on the left side about have way between your navel and your left side. Wrap it around your belt and now you have identified where the loop must go. Remember be sure that your belt and pants are at the level you want them to be. Now the next step could be a bit hard to do but it is actually quite simple. Keeping the belt loop in the area you want it to be take the entire belt off your belt and take it back to your sewing area. Place that 2" cardboard spacer into the belt loop. Cut the belt so that the end forms a 2" loop then use the lighter or matches to melt the end of the cut so that it does not fray.

Before you start to sew the loop together like the first loop be sure the belt loop is on the same side of the belt as the other loop. That makes the belt look a lot neater when it is on.

One more suggestion here. When you are working building the BAT BELT try and do it someplace where you have good lighting someplace to sit and a good space on a table. And someplace without a TV or computer on or people bugging you. It just makes it easier to concentrate on what you are doing so you can do the job the correct way and end up with a product that will last a surprisingly long time.

Now I have given you good details on how to do each step and the key thing is to follow them. Now after you complete them all you might discover a better way and thats fine and I would appreciate it if you told me about it so I could add it to our next edition.

When you follow these directions you will make an excellent Bat Pender that will last you for years and probably forever!

YOU HAVE JUST COMPLETED BUILDING YOUR BAT PENDER!!!! CONGRADUALTIONS

See how compact the BAT PENDER is! Yet this very efficient device

prevents your pants from falling down!

STEP SEVEN

You have completed it so now you need to become familiar with using it! It is actually much easier to put on than a standard suspender. It is more comfortable and there are no metal clamps to scratch you or bend or slip off. And YOU made it.

You will discover that the area on your belt where you attach your BAT PENDER will determine how well it works and once you have discovered the best spots to put it you will see what I mean.

POSSIBLE PROBLEMS

Life is wonderful and every day is a gift but unfortunately there are also problems you had better try your best to solve!

The only problem I discovered is that with certain pants especially the ones make in China the belt loops may not securely sewn onto the pants and so any upward force on your belt by your BAT PENDER will exert force on the belt loops possibly causing them to break free from your pants. The easy fix if this occurs is simply to place a few thread stitches in the belt loops. In nearly every case there are no problems and usually the belt loops are securely sewn on the pants.

You also need to take care where you place the belt. For example if you place the front loop too far to the left side and the back belt too close to the spine then you will likely place too much stress on the horizontal belt and that will cause the pants to be pulled up unevenly at the back. So try and find the best locations for the Bat Pender and once you find them problem solved! And once you have no problems and you are happy you might consider going on a diet like I did to lose some weight. But that is anohter story.

Remember that a standard suspender may allow you to not have a belt. Not in all cases but it is possible in some cases especially if you sew buttons onto your pants. The BAT PENDER requires a belt because it is attached to the belt and keeps the belt and pants elevated. I will try and make that a bit clearer. The Bat Pender is designed to work WITH a belt not without a belt.

One potential problem with the BAT PENDER is that it may require some adjustment with different types of pant styles. Some pants ride lower or higher and in most cases you can adjust for that simply by increasing or decreasing the position of the Bat Pender on your belt placing it further to the side or closer or farther from your spine.

There is also an option. I suggest using non elastic nylon or rayon webbing. But you could also use elastic webbing if you wish. And if you wanted to you could place a metal adjusting buckle on the Bat Pender so that you could adjust it's length. I don't really think that is necessary but you may find it a useful option. I suppose you could use an old belt for parts. But is nearly all cases I don't think it would be necessary. Your call.

ADDITONAL USES FOR THE BAT PENDER

When I was researching the Bat Pender to see if anyone else every used a design that was a bit simiar I discoved something our Royal Canadian Mounted Police used on their dress uniforms to help hold up their gun holsters!

While they had some similarities in that their belts traveled at an angle across their chests they were not used to fasten to ther belts to keep their pants up!

It really is surprising how you can use this device. The standard use is to keep you pants from falling down! But if you took it off you now have a belt with a loop on each end that you can use for other purposes. If for example you placed one end of the belt through the loop at the other end now you have a device to secure something in place. And it gets even more interesting.

If you were floating in the water with the BAT PENDER on somebody could reach down from a boat and grab the back of your Bat Pender and pull you onboard! Then you wouldn't drown. How cool is that? Not drowning is a good story and basically somebody needs something to pull when they try and get you our of the water.

And there are a few other interesting things you can do! I suggested a black color for the belt but you could use white or red or blue or possibly even camo if you could find one. Depending on which color clothing you wear the color of the belt will look even better! If for example you use a black Bat Pender on a black T-shirt you can hardly see the Bat Pender but if you used the same color on a white T-shirt it would stand out much more. In most cases your shirt or sweater will cover your Bat Pender but if not the correct color would help you look better. In any event you will look much better than having one of those traditional ugly suspenders on. Yuck.

If you wanted to carry a spare key for you residence or car or whatever you could afix it to the BAT Pender. So you would always have a spare copy in a safe place.

One of the problems with "stuff" is that we tend to carry too much of it wherever we go and we tend to plaee it into our pockets. And sometimes we forget to place the stuff in our pockets. In unfortunate cases somebody comes up behind us and slips their hands into our pockets and grabs whatever they can.

But if you somehow figured out how to attach the "stuff" to your BAT PENDER the story would change to your advantage. Not all of it would fit but in most cases you could add a little packet sewn onto the BAT PENDER to hold say your passport or credit card or whatever. There are opportunities here! A bit more sewing but so what!

When YOU make something you are in control. Somebody else is not doing it for you. Somebody else is not charging you all sorts of money for it over the actual cost of the materials. I once checked out the price for new roof and discovered that they charged twice as much as the cost of the actual materials.

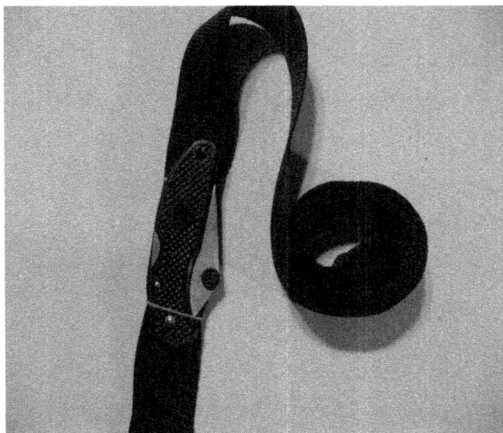

Just to show you what I mean here is a flip open knife with a 2½ inch blade that I purchased at a Dollar Store for $1.50 held on to the belt with two elastic bands. You could sew on a small pouch if you wished. You could sew just about any slim device onto your BAT PENDER and it would be readily accessible to you anytime.

If you wanted to carry a personal protection device or even a Swiss army knife you could attach that to the front or back of your BAT Pender. That would be pretty easy to do as you could sew a small bit of webbing on the belt to hold the device. It could even be a small flashlight the ones that have the lithium bulbs and very bright lights.

I would suggest that you not attempt to board a plane with that equipment but anywhere else would be fine. On the plane you would be arrested and you would blame me. But you could also place the suspicious stuff in your luggage and after you got your luggage back after the flight you could put it back on you BAT PENDER. Or if you wanted to you could simply buy some more stuff once you landed. So there are good answers to this potential get arrested on a plane problem.

I will give you another very clever idea for the Bat Pender. I have tried this and it works! All you need to do is locate a small camera pouch with a belt loop on the back. Some of them have a belt loop snap fastener so that you can open up the loop and they would be the best. You can use that as a device to carry whatever you wanted to carry and not only that you can carry it at belt level if you wish or higher up. You can easily pick these things up for a couple of dollars at thrift stores and Dollar Stores and not only is it fun to look it also gives you a chance to get the best size and quality.

I hope that your BAT Pender works well for you too! When I invented it I realized that I could have them manufactured and sell them but I also considered that actually it would be a lot more fun to make them yourself and not only that you could make them at the precise size that would fit you best. Not only would it cost you less to make them yourself you would also have more fun doing it! And when you make something and have fun you feel happy. So I want you to be happy. If you are happy so am I and if everyone is happy the BAT PENDER is doing what I wanted it to do! Maybe I should have called it the HAPPY PENDER?

And I have another theory too. A lot of the manufactured goods made today are purposely made cheaply so that they wear out and you need to buy more of them over time. In the old days one could buy a Hudson's Bay wool blanket that would last for your entire life and your kids lives too!. Today you tend to purchase cheap blankets made in China that wear out after a couple of years. They do the same with pens. In the old days you could buy a quality Parker Pen made in the USA that would last for decades and all you had to do was replace the refill once every two years or so. But today you can buy cheap pens for China in the dollar store and they break in a few weeks

and you need to replace them
with new pens. I should stop here
but I won't. We do have a big
problem today with
manufacturing in other countries.

Now lets consider car
manufacturers. When they make
a car they want the outside to look
good and the interior to look
good. So you look at it and take it
for a test run and then you buy it.
Lets say that you finance the car
via a bank loan. It will take you
on average 65 months or 5.5 years
to pay it off. So how does the car
company design the car? First of
all they design it so that there are
no mechanical problems for the
first three years. The main reason
is they need to provide you with a
guarantee and they don't want to
pay for the repairs themselves.
And if the damn car breaks that

quickly you will blab to all your friends and they won't buy one either.

But then for the next 2.5 years small problems begin to occur. You will need to replace your windshield wipers, your battery and your brake pads. Not a lot of expense but what that does is alert you that your car is beginning to age. Lights will begin to burn out. Then the magic starts to happen. Your water pump may fail as you approach the 6th or 7th year. And the company has designed the pump to be expensive to change. The part itself may only be $100 or $200 but putting it in might cost you another $200 or even more. Trust me I have replaced water pumps on my vehicles and what should be a simple repair is made time consuming by the

Engineering rascals who designed it for that purpose. This makes good revenue for the dealers of the Car company. Then you need brake rotors and again although the parts are not that expensive having them installed can cost you several hundred extra dollars.

So what is happening is that the maintenance costs on your car are steadily increasing and you suddenly begin to think about getting a new vehicle. And my point here is that the consumer is being ripped off! The damn car or truck was designed with these parts so that these very events would in fact happen and the owner would begin to consider the advantages of getting a replacement vehicle.

And this is not just cars and trucks. The same process is used by companies that manufacture other products. So there are huge advantages in building items yourself. Because of the complexity and technology associated with many items building them yourself is often not an option but in the case of the BAT PENDER you now have a choice.

Not only can you build it yourself at a much lower cost than buying a traditional suspender you can also ensure that it is built to a very good quality standard so that you can use it as long as you wish! Imagine making your Bat Pender in say 2018 and having it still working perfectly in 2068. I would be 120 years old then so that seems a bit unlikely so it would be nice if you thanked me much sooner!

But in the case of the BAT PENDER once you build it it should outlast any suspender you may have bought in China. So my point here is that there are advantages to making things yourself to a good quality level. They make great gifts. They should last for decades and you will even save money too!

And another advantage is that making the BAT Pender will take you away from your cell phones and computer and TV set and allow you to actually make something useful. You don't need to pay high prices and add tax to that and you can actually learn a few things about how to sew! And surprisingly you may start to consider other alternatives rather than lining up at the store every time to give them all your money.

MODIFICATIONS TO YOUR BAT PENDER

After you build your BAT PENDER you also have several possible modifications that you can make. If you want to.   You could change the color so that this device looks better with the type of clothes you are wearing at the time.

Although the BAT PENDER does require a belt if you really want to you could simply make two of them and at the back where they would cross each other you could sew both together and place a small piece of leather over it. If you do that you will not need a belt because you will have four attachment points for your revised Bat Penders onto your pants. So instead of the loops at each end of the penders you would need to sew on some leather pieces with button holes in them and place buttons on your pants where you want the pender to attach.

This does sound like more work and it is but it would be possible to do this and actually although it would take some more time it would not be that difficult. And there is an option here too. If you wanted two pender belts but still wanted to wear a regular belt around your waist you could keep the original belt loops on your BAT Pender. Never say that you "can't do that" as there are always ways of doing just about anything!

As you can see there are options here. You could also sew some sort of design items on your Bat Penders. A flag or character or whatever and you can often purchase them at a dollar store for a very reasonable price. Now consider this idea. At this point you have followed the directions and built the Bat Penders yourself.

You are not going to a store and purchasing them or finding them online in a business from China and ordering them. You have taken charge! You are the builder. So actually if you wish to change the design a bit or add to it that is entirely up to you. And as I mentioned earlier here is an opportunity to think outside the box. Trust me there will be some people who will make fun of you.

Just laugh at them. Ask them if they have made anything?

There are lots of options. I suggest that you hand sew the Bat Pender but what if you have access to a sewing machine or a Mom or friend with one. It would take about five seconds to do each Bat Pender loop with a sewing machine. By hand it took me about 15 minutes to do both ends. If I was going to make more than one I would use a sewing machine.

If I was going to make a few hundred of them for resale I would not use a bic lighter to melt the ends of the belts before sewing. I would used a faster method. If I was gong to make a lot of them instead of going to a fabric store and purchasing a few feet of nylon or rayon webbing I would find a less expensive source where one could purchase a entire roll or two at a time. In higher quantities I could likely bring the production costs down by say 75% or more. So there are lots of options depending on what you want to do.

Speaking of options and understanding how life really works and doing fun stuff and things like that you might also wish to read some of our books. Now some of you might not like this book and I understand that. I learned early as a Publisher that when you publish ANY book some will love it and the trolls and haters will do nothing but complain about it. They can't help it so no problem.

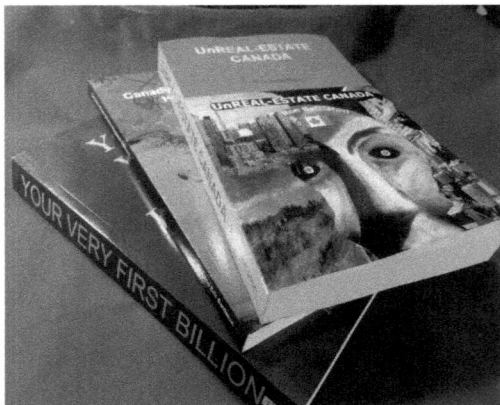

One of the objectives of our Publishing company Battiston Publishing which I started back in 1996 was to show our readers what was actually going on. How to save money and live a happier and safer life. You might enjoy our books. You might not.

Here are three books that you just might like. Your Very First Billion, The Canadian Winter Drivers Handbook ed 2 and UnReal-Estate Canada. Our objective is to show you accurate information that helps you live a better and happier life and not all are necessarily politically correct. Because when you do that often the message does not get out.

If you have any suggestions or if you are looking for a Publisher for your own manuscript I would be happy to hear from you. I can be contacted at the following e-mail accounts and websites. If you wish to manufacture the Bat Pender for commercial use just contact me and I am sure that we can arrive at a good deal.

My main objective is to share the Bat Pender idea with people who will enjoy using it and who will make it themselves!

ron@BatPender.com

ron@BattistonPublishing.com

BatPender.com

BattistonPublishing.com

Cheers!

Ron Battiston

BatPender.com

BattistonPublishing.com

www.ingramcontent.com/pod-product-compliance
Lightning Source LLC
Chambersburg PA
CBHW071844020426
42331CB00007B/1849